> Your country has the right to your service…you cannot decline the burdens…and still expect to share its honor.
>
> —Pericles, 430 B.C.[1]

Pericles' profound imperative to the political class of Athens rings eerily similar to the current debate over the nature of the all-volunteer force that is fighting our nation's wars. The relationship between the nation and its all-volunteer force has senior political and military leaders extremely concerned. Has our all-volunteer force grown away from the larger U.S. society? This perceived separation poses grave dangers for the long-term health of U.S. forces and of the nation. During an address at West Point, former Joint Chiefs of Staff Chairman Admiral Mike Mullen expressed his anxiety over the "widening and worrisome divide" between the U.S. military and our society at large.[2] Former defense Secretary Robert Gates echoed this apprehension during his final address at West Point: "A civil-military divide can expose itself in an ugly way, especially during a protracted and frustrating war effort."[3]

This strategic research project (SRP) examines two distinct but related divides between the nation's military and the civilian society. Specifically, it addresses the chasm between the junior ranks of the military and civil society, and concurrently addresses the civil-military disconnect between senior officers and the political class. It reviews the current narrative and analyzes the beliefs, values, and demographics which contribute to these divides, then speculates on the root causes of these disconnects and concludes by suggesting that military leaders and political elites share a responsibility to narrow these gaps for the sake of the nation and the health of its fighting force.

Current Narrative

Throughout much of U.S. history the nation's Soldiers, Airmen, Sailors, and Marines have embodied the conscience of American Society. Since the turn of the 21st century, Americans have expressed a deep appreciation and profound respect for our military. A 2010 Gallup poll suggests that the military remains the most admired institution in America; an overwhelming number of U.S. citizens (76%) hold the military in a higher regard than all other national institutions.[4] Despite the military's loss of 6 percentage points from the previous year, no other institution came within 10 percentage points of our military in the survey. Oddly, the military's continued popularity seems as a peculiar trend because the military is the nation's least democratic institution.[5] Thomas Owens describes this narrative in *U.S. Civil-Military Relations After 9/11: Renegotiating the Civil-Military Bargain,* as "…somewhat unseemly for democratic people to hold arguably the least democratic institution in America in much higher regard than the most democratic—the U.S. Congress."[6]

However, one conundrum often overlooked in surveys affirming the public's admiration for our military is the apprehension between a citizen's genuine gratitude towards the military member for their service, and the guilt that citizens may feel for not sharing the burdens of service. Some U.S. civilians feel guilty because only a few face the demanding realities of defending our nation. Perhaps these non-serving citizens feel an overwhelming indebtedness to our Soldiers. Few U.S. citizens endure the rigors of combat, yet most enjoy some comfort and a sense of security in their daily lives thanks to the all-volunteer force.[7] Conceivably this contributes to and to some degree explains a feeling of resentment among the military towards the civilians. In some cases, Soldiers may feel that the dangerous realities they face in combat are not completely understood by the average U.S. citizen. "You can't handle the truth!" bellowed Marine Colonel Nathan Jessup, a fictional character played by Jack Nicolson in the 1992 motion picture *A Few Good Men*.[8] This well-known movie dramatizes professional Soldiers belief that some Americans do not want to deal with the harsh truths of war that the U.S. military deals with on a daily basis.[9] The counter-argument to this fictional depiction is the fact that these Soldiers, Sailors, Airmen, and Marines all volunteered— hence the "all-volunteer force." How can you volunteer for love of country and then resent the very citizens of the country you serve?

In recent years, when a uniformed Soldier walks through the nation's airports, many citizens respectfully display or voice their gratitude. Perhaps this gratitude coupled with guilt is compounded by the discomforting legacy of the Vietnam War, when many young Americans expressed their opposition to the Vietnam War.[10] In an article titled: "On War, Guilt and "Thank You for your Service" Elizabeth Samet, author and West Point professor, notes that a Soldier in uniform walking the streets of New York "constitutes a spectacle." She reports that Soldiers in uniform get "bombarded with gratitude."[11] Citizens offer the obligatory "Thank you for your service." Samet believes that "Thank you for your service" has become a "mantra of atonement."[12] She infers that some U.S. citizens rely on such expressions of gratitude as a way of alleviating their guilt for not sharing the burden of securing the nation.[13] Samet's analysis highlights a perceptual gap and lack of mutual understanding between the civilian population and military service members. Indeed, the average citizen has little if any contact with service members. Samet further notes that this expression of appreciation "has circumvented a more enduring human connection that doesn't bode well for mutual understanding between Soldiers and civilians."[14]

It seems counter-intuitive to describe the public's empathies and admirations for the nation's military…and then to question the military's relationship with society. Indeed, history reveals a natural divide in the cultures of a liberal society and its military. Samuel Huntington in the book *The Soldier and the State,* eloquently describes this narrative: "For the liberal, success in any enterprise depends upon maximum release of individual energies; for the military man it depends on subordination and specialization. The liberal glorifies self expression, the military man obedience."[15] Even so, such a society must remain aware of the sacrifices inherent with military service.

The nation's all-volunteer force, particularly the Army and Marines, pay a vast price for fulfilling the nation's security requirements across the globe. Beyond their casualties in the wars in Iraq and Afghanistan, U.S. Soldiers and Marines contribute an enormous personal price at home for their service. High rates of post-traumatic stress, divorce, and suicide result from exposure to intense ground-combat experience.[16]

Compared to previous times in our history an increasing percentage of U.S. society seems unaware of the missions and sacrifices of the nations all-volunteer force.[17] A common observation among Soldiers declares "The Army's at War and the rest of America is at the mall." The military's solution to troop strength shortages due to the massive deployments in Iraq and Afghanistan over the past nine years has been to extend overseas tours and enlistment terms for a vast majority of Soldiers.[18] A popular and broadly distributed photo in Iraq shows an Army Reservist's military vehicle with this sign on the windshield: "One weekend a month my ass!"[19] By 2010 as many as 13,000

Soldiers had served three or four combat tours in Iraq or Afghanistan.[20] Christopher Hammer, a military historian at George Mason University, said it well: "You've got the vast majority of the American military-aged population that is being asked to do virtually nothing in these two conflicts. And then a very small percentage is being asked to shoulder enormous burdens."[21]

The average Soldier or Marine is indeed playing varsity for the nation: among the nation's 18 to 24 year-olds, only 2 of 10 qualify for military service. The contribution of those who do choose to serve speaks volumes for their moral courage and patriotism. Yet the nation's continuing reliance on these few volunteers may be setting a dangerous precedent. Our young warriors may, with some justification, lay claim to moral superiority; they may feel estranged from their non-serving counterparts.[22] Former Secretary of Defense Robert Gates confirmed this when he spoke of the growing disconnect between the military and society in his reference to the "uniformed side of the equation."[23] Gates' use of the mathematical metaphor contributes to the broader narrative that, since the inception of the all-volunteer-force, our military has truly become a professional military. Arguably this transition to a professional military began at the conclusion of WWII. Nonetheless, members of our armed forces are citizens, but these professional volunteers do give up some rights to serve in the military. George Washington advised: "When we assumed the Soldier we did not lay aside the citizen." Our first President sought to assure that U.S. Soldiers are citizens first. In his democratic vision, no American would be purely a professional Soldier.[24] Therein lies the problem. As this analysis indicates, comparatively few Americans have served in the military since the inception of the all-volunteer force. During the Vietnam War 25% were draftees; similarly during WWII, 66% were draftees.[25] The difficulty is not that we don't have enough citizen volunteers to fill our ranks, rather that not enough citizens comprehend or identify with the military and those who served do not come from a proportional cross section of society. Has the professionalization of the military contributed to the broad divide within our nation? Perhaps this dilemma to some degree contributes to the civil-military tension between senior military leaders and political leaders.

Consider the number of veterans serving in the current Congress. Only 118 members (21%) have served or are currently serving in the military.[26] This represents a huge decline compared to other times in our history. During the 96th Congress (1979-1981), 298 congressmen were veterans, compared to 398 veterans from the 91st Congress (1969-1971).[27] Many of the veterans in the 91st Congress were instrumental in passing the 1973 War Powers Resolution, requiring the President to consult Congress before introducing U.S. forces into hostilities.[28] These Congressmen understood the magnitude of the political decision to send our sons and daughters to war. As fewer and fewer of our elected leaders have served in the military, it seems that these non-veteran politicians are more willing to support military incursions. Ironically, the War Powers Resolution coincides with the end of the draft in 1973. *Time Magazine*'s Mark Thompson indicates why this narrative is relevant: He believes the current Congress' lack of military experience limits legislators' ability to provide insightful and determined oversight of the military budget process.[29]

The nation's decision to rely on a professional all-volunteer military has inevitably contributed to a significant separation of our military from the society as a whole, so our military is not socio-economically or culturally representative of our society. We have no draft to ensure that all segments of society participate in the nation's wars. Thus the simple concept of an all-volunteer force contributes to the divide.

Former Secretary Gates and former Chairman Mullen's remarks on the "widening and worrisome divide" is not the first time in recent history that senior military or political leaders have articulated this concern. In 1997 Secretary of Defense William Cohen declared in a speech at Yale University that he perceived a "chasm' between the civilians and the rank-and-file of the military.[30] The late Joint Chiefs Chairman General John Shalikashvilli likewise observed: "I share deeply the concern that we are living through a period when the gap between the American people and their military is getting wider."[31] The media and some national defense publications similarly addressed the widening gap between the U.S. Military and society during the Clinton Administration. Tom Ricks'1997 *Atlantic Monthly Journal* article "The Widening Gap between the Military and the Society" provides an example by describing a Marine platoon's boot camp experience at Paris Island. Ricks concluded that a cultural transformation occurs during the boot camp experience—the transition from citizen to Marine.[32] Ricks believes this transition renders Marine veterans as outsiders when they re-enter society.[33] But Ricks' observations on the gap were based on the 1990s. He perceived a massive cultural difference between the military and U.S. society that was significantly different from that of other times in the nation's history. Ricks overarching argument focused on the professionalization of the military. He argued that the Marine culture of teamwork and discipline contrasted sharply with the values of a disjointed and individualistic society. Similarly, his portrayal inferred that the Marines promote this view of society during the inculcation process of boot camp.

Ricks later asserted that the officer corps appeared to be less representative of society and had an "open identification with the Republican Party."[34] Ricks' analysis has served as the foundation for the current analysis of the civil-military divide.

Indeed, Ricks' 1990's observations were perceptive and revealing. However, they did not anticipate the complexities of today's narrative. In the late 1990s, our Soldiers and Marines were not involved in the daily dangers of combat, and though the 1990s military was widely respected, Soldiers were not accorded the same reverence they get today. Even so, Ricks aptly indentified the lack of understanding between the beliefs and values of the military and those of the broad U.S. society.

Beliefs and Values

The military's political beliefs have deep roots in American history. The perception of a "Republicanization" of the military runs deep in American history. Indeed several episodes reveal the military's inclination to support the Republican Party. The first instance occurred during the American Civil War. The Copperheads or the "Peace Democrats" were an outspoken group of Northern Democrats who opposed the Civil War. Republicans referred to these Democrats as Copperheads, likening them to poisonous snakes.[35] These Democrat Copperheads constantly ridiculed Republican Abraham Lincoln and the war itself.[36] Union Soldiers perceived the Copperheads' hatred of Lincoln as an assault on their personal sacrifice and a detractor of the Union's war effort. The significance of this perception caused many Union Soldiers to become staunch Republicans in post-Civil War America.[37] A similar narrative developed after the Vietnam War.[38] The liberal anti-war movement left many returning veterans feeling bitter and "betrayed."[39] This view was later validated when a large number of Vietnam veterans opposed the 2004 Presidential candidacy of Democrat John Kerry.[40] Veterans perceived Kerry's 1973 testimony to the Senate Foreign Affairs Committee as an assault on their service.[41] Even if the professional military has beliefs and affiliations with the Republican Party, would these partisan beliefs affect their best professional advice to their civilian superiors on national security matters?

During the run-up to the Iraq War in 2003, Republican Secretary of Defense Donald Rumsfeld openly ridiculed senior military leaders counsel on the number of troops needed for the invasion and follow-on offensive operations. Conventional wisdom held that the military elite would march lock-step with the Republican Party. Nowhere was this conventional wisdom more wrong than during Army Chief of Staff General Eric Shinseki's testimony before Congress in the run-up to the Iraq War. Shinseki tacitly disagreed with the Bush Administration's estimate of troop strength needed to successfully prosecute the war in Iraq. Deputy Secretary of Defense Paul Wolfowitz would later disparage Shinseki's approximation as "wildly off the mark."[42] Wolfowitz's censure had a "chilling effect" on senior military officers.[43] The Administration's civilian establishment at the Pentagon eventually prevailed in this dispute over troop strength. Regardless of the fact that Shinseki's advice would later prove accurate, civilian supremacy over the military just as our fore fathers mandated won the day. Nevertheless, a few senior military leaders were infuriated at the Bush Administration.[44] Marine Lieutenant General Greg Newbold, Director of Operations for the Joint Staff, voiced his dissent during the planning stages of the war and then retired from active duty.[45] Newbold later wrote a scathing article in *Time Magazine,* criticizing former Secretary of State Condoleezza Rice and former Defense Secretary Donald Rumsfeld.[46]

The controversial relationship between national security civilians in the Bush Administration and the U.S. military from 2002 to 2006 were readily apparent to the rank and file of the military. A 2006 *Military Times* poll reported that almost 60 percent of the military did not believe that civilians in the Pentagon had their "best interests at heart."[47] Not only was a civil-military divide developing between the senior military brass and the Bush Administration, but it was also trickling to the junior ranks of the services.

Then an intriguing circumstance evolved; while senior military leaders were at odds with the Bush administration, the Democratic Party endured a "copperhead effect" during the Iraq war from 2003 to 2008. Similar to perceptions of the Copperheads from the Civil War, the disdain and criticism from the Democrats and the media during the height of the Iraq War were not directed at the rank and file of the military; rather they targeted policies of the Bush administration. As in the Civil War, Democrats' condemnation came at a time when U.S. Soldiers were suffering the ravages of improvised explosive devices (IEDs) and suicide bombers. Soldiers viewed these rhetorical condemnations from the Democrats as an assault on their personal sacrifices, and a detractor of the Iraq war effort.

To make matters worse, MoveOn.org's full-page *New York Times* ad portrayed a war-mongering Petraeus ("General Petraeus or General Betray US?") in response to his 2007 Congressional testimony on the progress of the surge in Iraq.[48] Incredibly, none of the 2008 Democratic Presidential candidates would go on record to denounce the "General Betray US" advertisement. Again the rank-and-file of the military witnessed firsthand a degrading treatment of one of their Commanding Generals. Ironically, a portion of U.S. public would later regard Petraeus as a hero because of the success of the Iraq surge.

Evidently, members of the U.S. military may remain skeptical about both political parties, regardless of their personal political beliefs. These recent civil-military clashes bring up the larger question of civilian control of the military. Does this question contribute to the military's divide with the broad society?

Samuel Huntington and Morris Janowitz have written extensively on this question. Huntington argued the nation should entrust the professional military to fight and win the nation's wars on their behalf.[49] Huntington further argued that the professional military's ethos should differ from that of the broad society it supposed to protect, especially the officer corps.[50] He viewed these attributes as essential to achieve our national security objectives.[51] In contrast, Janowitz stressed assimilation of the civilian and military institutions.[52] He viewed the senior military officer as the "warrior-scholar-statesmen," skilled in both politics and warfare.[53] Furthermore, Janowitz warned against abolishing conscription; he contended that an all-volunteer force could divert a Soldier's allegiance from the citizens they are supposed to protect.[54] In this decade of wars fought by a stressed all-volunteer force, has the military become what Huntington "advocated" and Janowitz "feared?"[55]

Certainly, the nation's professional military leaders become distressed when their civilian leaders ignore their best judgments on the application of military power.[56] However, a deeper divide in the future may not reside in these differences in political beliefs—but in differing religious beliefs. Have the religious beliefs of the all-volunteer force created a chasm between some secular citizens? Michael Lindsay, a Sociologist at Rice University, believes that American evangelicals have become prominent players within the U.S. military establishment. He claims this trend began with the transition from conscription to the all-volunteer force, at which time the military adopted a "conservative ethos."[57] Military recruits increasingly volunteered from a segment of society that had a strong cultural affiliation with the military lifestyle and conservative values.[58] Likewise, military recruiters drew heavily from parts of the country where evangelicalism was the norm. They "sold" a lifestyle that stressed respect for authority, discipline, family values, and a commitment to a higher cause.[59] Lindsay also offers evidence that as the all-volunteer force developed, our military commissioned a disproportionate percentage of evangelical chaplains.[60] Indeed by 2005, the Southern Baptist Convention was the largest source of military chaplains. Although only 1% of military members claimed membership in Southern Baptist churches, 16% of their chaplains were Southern Baptist.[61]

This evangelical trend dramatically captured national attention in 2002, when Lieutenant General Jerry Bokin delivered a sermon in uniform condemning "Islamic Satanists" at the First Baptist Church of Broken Arrow, Oklahoma. The former Delta Commander of the infamous Mogadishu raid, described in *Black Hawk Down,* declared to the congregation that "I knew my God was bigger than his. I knew my God was a real God and his was an idol."[62] Bokin then boasted of his capture of Osman Atto, a Muslim insurgent in Mogadishu.[63]

The nation's other military services have also exhibited such evangelical influences. Michael L. "Mickey" Weinstein, a former Judge Advocate in the Air Force and founder of the *Military Religious Freedom Foundation*, is an outspoken critic of the Christian influence on Air Force Academy cadets in Colorado Springs. In his objections to Air Force officers', chaplains', and Christian cadets' zealous imposition of their beliefs on non-Christian cadets, Weinstein contends the influence is unconstitutional.[64] Weinstein claims that organizations like the Officers' Christian Fellowship, the Christian Military Fellowship and the Christian Embassy exercise undue influence on the Academy's young cadets.[65] Obviously, religious beliefs have a significant impact and play an enormous role on the values of the all-volunteer force.

U.S. military values may provide the greatest insight into the current question of the divide with American society. Countless factors shape the military's values as demonstrated in the previous examples. Carl Builder, in *The Masks of War,* contends that the military as an institution "while composed of many ever-changing individuals, have distinct and enduring personalities of their own that govern much of their behavior."[66] Even though *The Masks of War* was published in 1989, Builders' theme is extremely relevant to today's values narrative. Builder notes that, while people change, institutional values endure. Each branch of service has unique norms and a formally established set of values. For example, the Army promulgates *The Seven Army Values*—loyalty, duty, respect, selfless service, honor, integrity, and personal courage. Likewise, the Marines espouse honor, courage, and commitment. In both cases, these values define the ideal service member's individual character and posit an uncompromising code designed to contribute to the overall professional ethos in the force.

Christopher Coker's *The Warrior Ethos: Military Culture and the War on Terror* attempts to assess the significance of service codes of values. Coker contends the warrior myth is not as captivating as it once was because U.S society is increasingly skeptical of the warrior's role. Further, the warrior's ethos has always been subordinated to that of the state.[67] Coker concludes that U.S. society wrongly assumes that our "democratic, liberal, and post modern beliefs" will guarantee our survival. In this era of persistent conflict and "suicide bombers," Coker believes we need the warrior's ethos more than ever.[68] Nonetheless, the nation's core values historically reflect the Judeo-Christian traditions.[69] These Judeo-Christian values have tremendous influence on the values of the U.S. military.[70] Charles Moskos affirmed this premise when he designated service in the nation's military as a "calling…transcending individual self-interest in favor of a presumed higher good."[71] Our service members' dedication to a higher good contributes to their higher "self-esteem." Likewise Moskos notes a close association with "self-sacrifice" and total commitment.[72] Judeo-Christian ideals surely influence the U.S. military's beliefs and values system. This dynamic may indeed contribute to the military's divide with the broad society. Religious differences between our military and our larger society have a regional and social class component. A disproportionate number of military members hail from the most conservative geographical areas of the country.

Current Demographics

The U.S. military has worked tirelessly to create a force that reflects the broad diversity of the U.S. population. The FY09 DoD report on social representation in the U.S. military indicates a broad mix of both racial and ethnic minorities and females serving in the Armed Forces, especially in the enlisted ranks.[73] The Navy has the largest percentage of non-whites serving in their enlisted force—40.1%.[74] In the other services, non-whites in the enlisted corps account for 31.0% of the Army, 28.5% of the Air Force, and 22.1% of the Marine Corps.[75] A report from the Military Leadership Diversity Commission further validates that the military has indeed created a racially and ethnically diverse force in the enlisted ranks.[76] However, the officer ranks tell a different story.[77] According to the same report, "the demographic composition of the officer corps is far from representative of the American population and…officers are much less demographically diverse than the enlisted troops they lead."[78] The report further indicates that whites account for 77% of the officer corps, compared to 66% of the U.S. population.[79] Conversely, blacks represent 8% of the officer corps, compared to 12% of the general population.[80] The greatest disparity in the officer corps resides with Hispanics: Hispanic citizens account for 5% of the officer corps, compared to 15% of the population.[81] The areas of the country where our service members volunteer from may provide some insights to the demographic disparities in the officer corps.

The regions of the United States from which we acquire our military recruits may provide the best explanation for the divide between our military and our society. The all-volunteer military is to a large degree "self-selecting".[82] Base closures and realignments have left most Army posts in Texas, Georgia, Kentucky, North Carolina, and Washington.[83] Base locations greatly influence the assumptions, beliefs, values and attitudes towards service most proximate to these military facilities.

Statistical analysis of population representation in the military from 1973 to 2009 indicates an interesting trend. The western and especially the southern region of the United States, play a disproportionate role in military accessions. These two regions account for 67% of military accessions in 2009, compared to 54% in 1973.[84] 2009 statistics indicate that the South provided the largest share of accessions at (43%), followed by the West at (24%), the North at (20%), and the Northeast at (13%).[85] In the West, the preponderance of volunteers comes from the Mountain-West and Mid-West. Likewise, across the country the preference to serve is most pronounced in rural areas and small towns—an inclination that goes beyond these communities share of the population as a whole.[86]

Socioeconomic status compounds this regional factor. Society's upper-class and upper-middle class are far less likely to contribute to the ranks of the military than the middle class.[87] A 2003 *New York Times* article described this dynamic in its assertion that our military "mirrors the working-class of America."[88] Of the first 28 Soldiers to die in the Iraq War, only one came from an upper-class family.[89]

Preparing our future officers for military duty, the service academies traditionally use a more structured approach to learning than that of the elite universities such as Harvard, Yale and Stanford. This approach over time, coupled with the conservative institutional values of the service academies, tend to produce a narrow foundation of cognitive diversity throughout the officer corps. Consequently, despite the military's tremendous efforts to achieve racial, ethnic, and gender equality, our military has failed to diversify the personality traits and cognitive characteristics of the force. Likewise, the bulk of ROTC accessions arrive from regions of the county where conservatism, Christianity, and other cultural factors are similar to those of service academy graduates. Universities such as Texas A&M, The Citadel, Virginia Military Institute, North Georgia College along with several other colleges in the South, Southwest, and

Midwest, contribute the greatest number of ROTC accessions to the military. Alabama, with a population of less than 5 million, hosts 10 ROTC programs, whereas the Chicago Metropolitan Area, with a population of 9 million, hosts only 3 ROTC programs.[90] While the officer accessions from these universities may be demographically diverse, the values, personality traits, and cognitive qualities of their graduates are remarkably similar.

So Where's the Divide?

This SRP speculates on four root causes of the divide. First, very few upper-class and upper-middle class citizens serve in the Armed Forces. Since the inception of the all-volunteer force, the U.S. military has leveraged "economic mobility"[91] tools such as the GI Bill, enlistment bonuses, ROTC scholarships, retirement benefits, and health care. Middle-class citizens have taken advantage of these programs. In many ways, our military mirrors our middle class. So the first divide is clearly between the upper classes of U.S. society and the middle-class.

Second, the divide is evident in the disproportionate regional distribution of volunteers for military service. As previously noted, very few volunteers come from the North, Northeast, and far Western portions of the nation. Indeed, the assumptions, values, and beliefs of citizens in the North, Northeast, and far Western portions of the country differ from those of citizens in the South, Southeast, and Midwest. From political preferences to religious affiliations, our military does not proportionally represent all regions of the country.

Third, 77% of the officer corps is white, compared to 66% of the population.[92] To further complicate matters, general officers and Navy admirals in the services are even whiter and more male.[93] As the Military Leadership Diversity Commission points out, several outliers contribute to this disparity: high turnover rates for women, fierce labor market competition for college-educated minorities, and exclusion of women from combat arms assignments.[94] Despite these explanatory factors, this disparity contributes to the divide.

Finally, the military's relationship with the political class has perhaps the most strategic implications. The professionalization of the military in the past four decades has contributed to this chasm. A 2007 Rand study indicates the military relies on a "pragmatist" and "realist" approach for solving national security problems. The Rand study finds that our military's organizational continuity and education system leads to "stable views" of national security issues.[95] In contrast, the nation's election cycles of every two to four years leads to a constant flow of new views, personalities, and ideas.[96] In some cases, these views can be profoundly different. This instability of views,[97] exacerbated by partisanship, endorsed or repudiated by media biases from both the left and the right, greatly contributes to the divide. *Time Magazine* describes a common feeling in the officer corps expressed by a Navy Captain who proclaimed that the U.S. political elites don't view the military as part of society, but "rather as their own private army."[98]

Narrowing the Divide

Our military and political leaders swear a similar oath to the U.S. Constitution. They also have an unwavering obligation to serve the American people. Perhaps, in a display of mutual cooperation, together our senior military officers and our political leaders could assist in narrowing the divide for the sake of the nation. Just as the civil-military divide has trickled down to the junior ranks, a renewed civil-military bond could unite them with the broad society.

First, our senior military leaders must reiterate to our young warriors that their

first responsibility is to serve as the nation's loyal and obedient servants, regardless of

their personal beliefs and values. Neither our drill sergeants nor our general officers,

who espouse these values, should use them as evidence of their moral superiority, and

hence of their loathing for the citizens they protect.

Second, our general officers should always demonstrate their commitment to

civilian control of our military. The revolt of Bush's Generals and General McCrystal's

staff inappropriate comments on the Obama administration reveal an unfortunate

departure from this civilian supremacy principle. Both of these cases reveal a total

dereliction of our military leaders' duty to this great republic.

Third, politicians from both political parties must assume mutual ownership with

our military for renewing our nation's civil-military bond. They should begin by adhering

to the principle that disagreement is not disrespect. Our nation requires a strong

professional military. When our senior military officers are called upon to render their

best professional advice, they should not be publically humiliated. In the past decade,

from the Republicans' disrespect of General Shinseki to the Democrats' contempt of

General Petraeus, both political parties have alienated our military and exacerbated a

troubled civil-military relationship. The American people deserve better. Finally, the

volatile complexities of global economics, Weapons of Mass Destruction proliferations,

the emergence of bellicose non-state actors, and the daily threats of terrorism all

contribute to a formidable security environment.

Military leaders and their civilian superiors can best serve and protect the nation

by addressing these critical issues in a trusting, constructive relationship. Our elected civilian leaders should remind themselves that Athens surrendered to Sparta a mere 25 years after Pericles' profound warning to the political class of Athens.

Endnotes

[1] Robert B. Strassler, The Landmark Thucydides: A Comprehensive Guide to the Peloponnesian War (New York, NY: Free Press 1996), 125.

[2] Thom Shanker, "At West Point, A Focus on Trust," *New York Times*, May 21, 2011.

[3] Robert M. Gates, "Thayer Award Remarks," October 6, 2011, linked from West Point Association of Graduates Home Page, "http://www.westpointaog.org/page.aspx?pid=4843" (accessed November 9, 2011).

[4] Lydia Sadeed, "Congress Ranks Last in Confidence in Institutions," July 22, 2010. http://www.gallup.com/poll/141512/Congress-Ranks-Last-Confidence-Institutions.aspx (accessed September 9, 2010)

[5] Mackubin Thomas Owens, *U.S. Civil Military Relations after 9/11: Renegotiating the Civil-Military Bargain* (New York, NY: The Continuum Publishing Group 2011), 129.

[6] Ibid.

[7] Rebecca L. Schiff, "The Military and Domestic Politics: A Concordance Theory of Civil Military Relations" (New York, NY: Routledge 2009), 5.

[8] Ibid.

[9] Ibid.

[10] Elizabeth Samet, "On War, Guilt and "Thank You for your Service," August 1, 2011. *Bloomberg*, http://www.bloomberg.com/news/2011-08-02/war-guilt-and-thank-you-for-your-service-commentary-by-elizabeth-samet.html (accessed September 10, 2011).

[11] Ibid.

[12] Ibid.

[13] Ibid.

[14] Ibid.

[15] Samuel P. Huntington, *The Soldier and the State: The Theory and Politics of Civil-Military Relations* (Campbridge, MA: The Belknap Press of Harvard University Press, 1957), 90.

[16] Michael E. O'Hanlon, "Who Will Fight for Us," Orbis 53, no. 3 (August 1, 2009): 405.

[17] Ibid., 406.

[18] Mathew J. Morgan, "American Empire and the American Military," *Armed Forces and Society* 32, no. 2 (January 2006): 213.

[19] Ibid.

[20] Gregg Zoroya, "Troops' Deployment Burden Unprecedented," USA Today, January 13, 2010.

[21] Ibid.

[22] Gregory D. Foster, "Civil-Military Gap: What are the Ethics?" *United States Naval Institute Proceedings* 126, no. 4 (April 2000): 83.

[23] Gates, Thayer Award Remarks, West Point Association of Graduates Home Page.

[24] Ibid.

[25] George Mastroianni and Wilbur Scott, "After Iraq: The Politics of Blame and Civil Military Relations," *Military Review*, (July-August 2008): 57.

[26] Jennifer E. Manning, *Membership of the 112th Congress: A Profile* (Washington, D.C. U.S. Libarary of Congress, Congressional Research Service, August 4, 2011), 7.

[27] Ibid.

[28] Library of Congress, Joint Resolution United States Code Title 50, Chapter 33, Sections 1541-48. http://loc.gov/law/help/war-powers.php (accessed January 12, 2012).

[29] Mark Thompson, "The Other 1%," *Time* (November 11, 2011): 39.

[30] Peter D. Feaver and Richard H. Kohn, "The Gap: Soldiers, Civilians and their Mutual Misunderstanding," *The National Interest* 61, (Fall 2000): 29.

[31] Foster, "Civil-Military Gap: What are the Ethics?", 84.

[32] Thomas D. Ricks, "The Widening Gap between the Military and Society," *The Atlantic Monthly* 280, no.1, (July 1997): 68.

[33] Ibid.

[34] Ibid., 72.

[35] Copperheads or Peace Democrats: The term Copperhead originated during the Civil War. Although the Democratic Party broke apart in 1860, during the secession crisis Democrats in the North were generally more conciliatory toward the South than were Republicans. They called themselves Peace Democrats; their opponents called them Copperheads because some wore copper pennies as identifying badges. Republicans thus referred to them as venomous snakes. http://www.civilwarhome.com/copperheads.htm (accessed January 13, 2012).

[36] Owens, *U.S. Civil Military Relations after 9/11,* 173.

[37] Ibid.

[38] Ibid.

[39] Mastroianni and Scott, "After Iraq: The Politics of Blame and Civil Military Relations," 54. Also see: Owens, *U.S. Civil Military Relations after 9/11,*173.

[40] Owens, *U.S. Civil Military Relations after 9/11,*174.

[41] Ibid.

[42] Michale C. Desch, "Bush and the Generals," *Foreign Affairs*, May/June 2007 [journal online]; http://www.foreignaffairs.org/20070501faessay86309/michael-cdesch/bush-and-the-generals.html; Internet; (accessed September 22, 2011).

[43] Suzanne C. Nielsen and Don M. Snider, *American Civil-Military Relations: The Soldier and the State in a New Era* (Baltimore, Maryland: The John Hopkins University Press, 2009), 110.

[44] Ibid.

[45] Lieutenant General Gregg Newbold (Ret.), "Why Iraq Was a Mistake," *Time*, April 09, 2006, 21.

[46] Ibid.

[47] Desch, "Bush and the Generals," *Foreign Affairs*, May/June 2007.

[48] "Liberal Demagogues Blast Petraeus and Surge," *Human Events*: 63, no. 61, (September 17, 2007), 3.

[49] Mastroianni and Scott, "After Iraq: The Politics of Blame and Civil Military Relations," 54.

[50] Ibid.

[51] Ibid.

[52] Ibid.

[53] Ibid.

[54] Ibid.

[55] Ibid.

[56] Morgan, "American Empire and the American Military," January 2006, 213.

[57] Michael D. Lindsey, "Evangelical Elites in the U.S. Military "*Journal of Political and Military Sociology* 35, no. 2 (Winter 2007), 164.

[58] Ibid.

[59] Ibid.

[60] Ibid.

[61] Ibid., 165.

[62] Commentary, "The Pentagon Unleashes a Holy Warrior," *Los Angeles Times*, October 16, 2003.

[63] Ibid.

[64] Amy Frykholm, "Christian Soldiers?" *The Christian Century,* 124, no 23 (November 13, 2007): 8.

[65] Ibid.

[66] Carl H. Builder, *The Masks of War: American Military Styles in Strategy and Analysis* (Baltimore, Maryland: The John Hopkins University Press, 1989), 3.

[67] Christopher Coker, *The Warrior Ethos: Military Culture and the War on Terror* (New York, NY: Routledge, 2007), 11.

[68] Ibid., 147.

[69] Clay T. Buckingham, "Ethics and the Military Officer: Institutional Tensions," *Parameters* 15, no. 1 (Autumn 1985): 23.

[70] Ibid.

[71] Charles C. Moskos Jr., "The All Volunteer Military: Calling, Profession, or Occupation?" *Parameters* 7, no.1 (Autumn 1977): 2.

[72] Ibid.

[73] Department of Defense, *"Population Representation in the Military Services Fiscal Year 2009 Report,"* October 1, 2009, Defense.gov,prhome.defense.gov/MPP/ ACCESSION%20POLICY/PopRep2009/summary/PopRep09Summ.pdf (accessed October 21, 2011).

[74] Ibid., 10.

[75] Ibid.

[76] Daniel Sagalyn, "PBS New Hour Report: U.S. Military Leadership Lacks Diversity at the Top" March 11, 2011. http://www.pbs.org/newshour/rundown/2011/03/military-report.html (accessed January 13, 2012) Also see: Military Leadership Diversity Commission, From Representation to Inclusion: Diversity Leadership for the 21st Century Military, (Arlington, VA March 15, 2011).

[77] Ibid.

[78] Ibid.

[79] Ibid.

[80] Ibid.

[81] Ibid.

[82] Gates, Thayer Award Remarks, West Point Association of Graduates Home Page.

[83] Ibid.

[84] *Department of Defense, "Population Representation in the Military Services Fiscal Year 2009 Report,": 11.*

[85] Ibid.

[86] Gates, Thayer Award Remarks, West Point Association of Graduates Home Page.

[87] William A. Galston, "Thinking About the Draft", Public Interest, 154, (Winter 2004): 69.

[88] Ibid.

[89] Ibid.

[90] Gates, Thayer Award Remarks, West Point Association of Graduates Home Page.

[91] Galston, "Thinking About the Draft", 69.

[92] Daniel Sagalyn, "PBS New Hour Report: U.S. Military Leadership Lacks Diversity at the Top":1.

[93] Ibid.

[94] Ibid.

[95] Thomas S. Sazanyna, Kevin F. McCarthy, Jerry M. Solinger, Linda J. Demaine, Jefferson P. Marquis, Brett Steele, *The Civil Military Gap in the United States: Does it Exist, Why, and Does it Matter?* (Arlington, VA: RAND Corporation, 2007) 156. Note: This study was published in 2007; however, it is important to note that the surveys were based on attitudes prior to the events of 9/11—so some of the data is not applicable to today's narrative.

[96] Ibid.

[97] Ibid.

[98] Thompson, "The Other 1%," 37.